Animal  Lives

ANTS

Sally Morgan

QEB Publishing

Published in the United States by
QEB Publishing, Inc.
23062 La Cadena Drive
Laguna Hills, CA 92653

www.qeb-publishing.com

Library of Congress Control Number: 2008011522

ISBN 978 1 59566 534 8

Written by Sally Morgan
Design and editorial by East River Partnership

Publisher Steve Evans
Creative Director Zeta Davies

Printed and bound in the United States

Picture Credits

Key: t = top, b = bottom, l = left, r = right,
c = center, FC = front cover

Alex Wild Photography 29tr; **Corbis**
/Anthony Bannister Gallo Images 8, 14,
/Tom Brakefield 24–25; **Ecoscene** /Ken
Wilson 10–11, 30br, /Wayne Lawler 20br,
/Robin Williams 30tr; **Getty** /Gail Shumway
6–7 /Mark Moffett 6bl; **Photolibrary** /Oxford
Scientific 12–13, 15; **Photoshot/NHPA** /Daniel
Heuclin 5br, /N A Callow 10cl, 11br, 30c,
/George Bernard 20–21, /Anthony Bannister
27, /Martin Harvey 28–29; **Shutterstock**
/Coco 1, /Marek Lambert 4–5, /Tan Hung
Meng 9, /D Morley Read 13tr, /Arteki 13br,
/Steve Shoup 16–17, /Pixelman 18, /Frank
B Yuwono 22bl, 30l, /Plastique 22–23, /JD
25br, /Tischenko Irina background 2–3, 8–9,
14–15, 18–19, 26–27, 30–31, 32.

Words in **bold** are explained
in the glossary on page 31.

Contents

Ants

Ants are extremely busy **insects** that live together in groups called **colonies**. There are more ants in the world than any other type of insect.

Powerful jaws

An ant's body is made up of three main parts called the head, the **thorax**, and the **abdomen**. On its large head, an ant has a pair of powerful jaws called **mandibles**, as well as two **antennae**. An ant uses its antennae for many things, including touching, smelling, and tasting. The ant has a very narrow waist between its thorax and abdomen and three pairs of legs. Its closest relatives are bees and wasps.

Ant fact!

Incredibly, the weight of all the ants in the world is equal to the weight of all humans.

Waist

Abdomen

Antenna

Head

Thorax

Leg

Ants have a head, a thorax, an abdomen, and six legs.

Workers and queens

Most ants in a colony are female, but there is one larger female, called the queen, that lays all the eggs. There are also male ants. The queen's eggs hatch into **larvae**, which then **pupate** and change into adults.

The weaver ant queen is huge compared to the tiny workers that live with her.

Types of ant

Scientists have named about 10,000 species, or types, of ant. However, there could be as many as 10,000 more species of ant still to be discovered.

Large and small

The largest ants of all are the driver ants, whose queens can be up to 2 inches long. The smallest ants are the tiny pharaoh ants. A pharaoh ant is no bigger than a grain of sand.

This harvester ant has found a large seed.

Hunters and harvesters

Ants are divided into groups according to what they look like, where they live, and the type of food they eat. Formica ants, for example, are ants that kill other insects and suck the juice from them. Leafcutter ants cut up leaves and carry bits back to their nest, while the harvester ants eat seeds.

These leafcutter ants are carrying bits of leaves back to their nest.

Where do you find ants?

Ants are very ancient animals. They have been around since the time of the dinosaurs, more than 100 million years ago.

Too cold for ants

Although ants can survive in hot deserts, they cannot live in very cold parts of the world, such as Antarctica, Iceland, and Greenland. Ants are also not found on some islands in the Pacific Ocean.

Some ants are able to live in dry deserts where there is almost no water.

Ant fact!

Desert ants can survive on the surface of hot sand that reaches temperatures of up to 158 degrees Fahrenheit.

Rain forest ants

Ants live in many different **habitats**, but the largest numbers are found in tropical rain forests. There are so many ants living in the Amazon rain forest that, if all the animals that live there were weighed, ants would make up one-third of the weight.

Huge numbers of ants live in the trees and on the ground of a rain forest.

Ant development

An ant passes through four stages while developing into an adult. These are the egg, larva, **pupa**, and adult stages.

Eggs

At just 0.5 millimeters long, many ant eggs are no bigger than pinheads. The eggs are moist and stick together, which helps worker ants carry them to safety if **predators** attack the nest.

The eggs and the pupae are cared for by nurse ants.

Eggs

Larva and pupa

After the eggs are laid by the queen, a larva emerges from each egg. This larva grows quickly to full size and then changes into a pupa. An adult ant develops inside each pupa. This change is called **metamorphosis**.

Larva

Ant fact!

All the worker ants in a colony have the same mother, the queen, so they are all sisters!

New colonies

When a colony becomes too large, the queen lays special eggs that grow into males and new queens. When they are ready, the males and queens form new colonies elsewhere.

Pupa

. eggs hatch
to maggot-
ke larvae.

Living together

Ants live in colonies of many different sizes, from small ones to extremely large ones. A colony of black ants, for example, contains about 4,000 ants, while a wood ant colony can have 300,000 or more ants. Some of the largest colonies are made up of many millions of ants.

There are three types of ant that live in a colony. These are the queen, the males, and the female workers. Most colonies only have one queen. Male ants, which are only found in the ant colony at certain times of year, mate with the queen and then they die.

Worker ants

Most ants in a colony are female workers that cannot lay eggs. The workers collect food, build the nest, look after eggs, and feed the larvae. Some of the workers, called soldier ants, have extra-large heads. They defend the colony and attack ants from other colonies.

This queen army ant has huge abdome and can lay thousands of eggs.

12

Soldier ants have huge jaws, which they use to attack predators.

Supercolonies

The largest ant colonies can cover a huge area. Argentine ants, which arrived in Europe about 80 years ago, have now formed a supercolony containing billions of ants. It stretches 3,700 miles along the coast from Italy to Portugal.

This female worker ant is taking a dead termite back to the nest.

Ant fact!

The African driver ant queen can lay as many as four million eggs in one month.

Building homes

Many ants make nests with rooms and tunnels. Some rooms are used as nurseries for larvae, others for storing food. Ants build their nests in different places. For example, carpenter ants carve out rooms and tunnels in rotting wood, while Aztec ants dig a hole for their nests in a living tree trunk.

Tailor ants stick leaves together to form a nest in a tree.

Devil's Garden

Lemon ants live in lemon ant trees in the rain forest. They kill almost all plants that are close to a lemon ant tree by injecting **formic acid** into their leaves. This creates a large area, called a Devil's Garden, which can contain more than 300 lemon ant trees and hardly any other plants.

Ant fact!

Tailor and weaver ants build their nests from leaves, which they glue together using a sticky thread made by their larvae.

This bivouac is a mass of living ants.

Bivouacs

Army and driver ants do not have a permanent nest. Instead, they build temporary nests called bivouacs. These nests are living nests as they are formed from a pile of worker ants! First, the ants find a branch just above the ground. Then the ants hold on to each other to form ropes under the branch. The ants form a thick curtain around the queen, eggs, and larvae.

Ant movement

An adult ant has six jointed legs that are attached to its thorax. These **agile** legs enable ants to move quickly. Army ants, for example, can cover 65 feet in an hour. That may not sound much, but to an ant, it is very fast!

When they are moving around, ants usually follow each other in a trail along the ground. They keep in contact by using their antennae to send and receive special messages.

Winged ants often emerge from the ground on warm summer evenings.

Flying ants

At certain times of year, lots of winged
ants appear above ground. These are the
new queens and males. They need wings
to fly away and find a place to start a new
colony. After a queen and male ant have
mated, the male dies. The queen then
chews off her wings and goes underground
to start laying eggs for the new colony.

Ant food

Ants eat many sorts of food, including seeds and rotting fruit that they find on the ground. Ants especially love sweet foods, such as sugar and **nectar**. Garden ants will often come into a house when they can smell sugar in the kitchen! Ants also feed on insects, small spiders, and tiny worms.

Squeezing out the juice

Ants cannot chew and swallow chunks of food. Instead, they use their powerful jaws to grip and squeeze the liquid out of the food. They then drink the liquid and leave the rest.

Some ants keep 'herds' of aphids that they milk to get a sugary juice called honeydew.

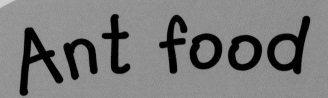

Two stomachs

Ants have two stomachs in their abdomen. They use the first stomach to store food that they carry back to the nest. They feed this food to the larvae and other ants in their colony. Food that goes into their second stomach is digested and used by the ant to feed itself.

Ant fact!

Leafcutter ants, which eat **fungus**, have underground fungal gardens. Fungus grows on the leaves that the leafcutter ants carry back to their nests.

The job of some honey ants is to drink and store as much nectar as possible for other ants. Their abdomen becomes so swollen that they cannot move.

Ant hunters

Driver ants in Africa and army ants in South America are two of the most feared types of ant. Each day, millions of these fierce ants swarm across the forest floor on hunting raids. Thousands of animals flee for their lives as a swarm approaches.

These ants are moving the body of a grasshopper back to their nest.

Some of these army ants are forming 'bridges' with their bodies so that other ants can march over them.

Ant attack

Driver ants and army ants attack any small animal in their path, including caterpillars, cockroaches, grasshoppers, and beetles. A large swarm of these ants may catch up to 100,000 tiny animals and insects in a single raid. African driver ants surround their **prey** and tear them to bits with their strong jaws. They even attack larger animals, such as chickens and cows, and carry the bits back to the nest!

Ant senses

An ant's most important sense organs are in their antennae. They use these for many things, including feeling and smelling. Ants also identify each other with their antennae. This lets them know if an ant they meet is from the same colony or not. By detecting smells in the air, antennae also help ants to find their way around.

Ants touch each other with their antennae when they meet.

Poor eyesight

Ants have a pair of compound eyes. This is a type of eye that is made up of lots of tiny eyes. But this does not mean that ants have good eyesight! In fact, the eyesight of many ants is poor. The driver ant, for example, is blind and has to find its way around using its sense of smell.

Ant enemies

An ant nest attracts a wide variety of predators, such as spiders, lizards, birds, and mammals.

Giant anteaters

The giant anteater is a large animal, so it takes a lot of ants to satisfy its hunger! After finding an ant nest, these animals use their powerful claws to rip open a hole. Then they lick up the ants with their long, sticky tongue, taking care to avoid the soldier ants. Giant anteaters can stick out their tongue about 150 times every minute! Other ant-eating animals include the aardvark, the armadillo, and the pangolin, which has an armored body covered in hard scales.

Eating parasites

Jays do not eat ants. Instead, these birds use ants to clean their bodies of parasites. To do this, a jay holds out its wings and allows them to swarm over its feathers. The ants remove any parasites and move on.

Birds feed ant eggs and pupae to their chicks.

Giant anteaters stick their long tongue into ant nests to lick up lots of ants.

Ant fact!

The sting of the bullet ant is so painful that when bitten, you may think you have been hit by a bullet!

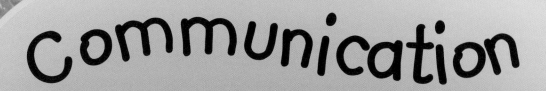

Communication

Ants communicate by touch and smell. They release scents called pheromones that other ants can smell. If an ant is crushed, its body releases a scent that warns other ants of danger. Sometimes, the scent of pheromones makes other ants attack.

Follow me

When ants have found a good food source, they lay down a trail of scent from the food back to the nest. This enables other ants to follow the trail to the food.

Soldier ants can detect the smell of an injured ant.

Ant fact!

Ant pheromones are so powerful that ants release just one billionth of a gram, a really tiny amount, when they want to communicate something to other ants.

Friend or foe?

All the ants from the same colony have the same smell. When they meet another ant, they smell it to see if it is a friend or an enemy. Ants from different colonies often fight, but sometimes they simply run away from each other.

A brave soldier ant attacks a much larger soldier termite.

27

Ants under threat

Most types of ant are not at risk. Some species are even thought of as pests. Carpenter ants, for example, can sometimes damage people's homes and leafcutters can ruin crops.

Disappearing forests

However, a few species of ant are now under threat. The dinosaur ant of Australia, which nests under eucalyptus trees, is becoming **endangered**. Many eucalyptus forests have been cut down or damaged by fire, destroying this ant's habitat. The dracula ant of Madagascar is another ant that is threatened by the loss of its forest habitat.

Ant fact!

The adult dracula ant cannot digest solid food. Instead, the larvae eat the food and then the adult sucks the larvae's blood!

Many different animals, including ants, lose their homes when forests are cleared.

Ants fighting ants

Some ant species are threatened by other ants. Aggressive Argentine ants, for example, have been introduced to many parts of the world, including Australia. These ants fight for food and space with local ants and drive them out.

The dinosaur ant of Australia was thought to be extinct until it was rediscovered in 1977.

Life cycle of an ant

A queen ant can start laying eggs when she is a few months old. She lays many thousands of eggs in her lifetime. Ants are the longest-living insects. Workers usually live for one year, but some can live for five years. Black ant queens have the longest life spans of 15 to 20 years. One queen lived in a German laboratory for 29 years.

Egg

Larva

Pupa in cocoon

Adult

Glossary

abdomen the third part of an insect's body, behind the thorax

agile describes a creature that can move quickly

antennae feelers that detect smells in the air

colony a group of animals, such as ants, living together

endangered animals that may become extinct if something is not done to protect them

formic acid a chemical that can burn when touched

fungus a type of mushroom that grows on rotting plants and animals

habitat the place in which an animal or plant lives

insect an animal with a head, thorax, abdomen, and three pairs of legs

larva the growing stage between the egg and the adult

mandibles an insect's jaws, used for biting and crushing food

metamorphosis the changes that take place in some animals between the larva and the adult stage

nectar the sugary liquid produced by many flowers

prey an animal that is hunted by other animals

predator an animal that hunts other animals

pupa the stage when a larva changes into an adult

pupate to go into the pupa stage

thorax the second part of an insect's body, joining the head to the abdomen

Index